Fergus Wilkie

St Andrews
PHOTOGRAPHS

fototank

To Isobel and David

The Photographs

St Andrews might be a town of modest size and population but it's an undisputed world leader in academia and golf, as well as one of the most attractive places in Scotland, with iconic beaches and ancient monuments. There's nowhere else like it.

University students, golfers, tourists and locals all add their own particular infusion of energy, against a backdrop of timeless nature and historic buildings. That's the essence of the place. It's the people that make St Andrews what it is: a vibrant, international, predominantly youthful, cultural centre.

Its natural assets might be a gift for the photographer, but St Andrews is also a place of continually changing elements that make capturing it on camera both enticing and challenging; photographing St Andrews means navigating – and exploiting – hugely variable tides, shifting sands, the impact of sunrise and sunset position, dramatic clouds, clear blue skies, haars, term time, golf season, January blues, long summer days and soft winter light.

My concept for a photography book about St Andrews was, first, to shoot a set of pictures specially for the purpose and, second, to present the photographs unencumbered by text, thereby achieving the fullest visual impact. I didn't want to follow the usual template of mixing pictures and text. Instead, additional information is gathered in a section of captions at the back of the book.

Since people are central to the theme, I have striven to include the human factor, whether as an element of a landscape, or more intimately via street photography.

The photographs flow from west to east, incorporating the key components of a multi-faceted town with people at its core, but they also flow in a sequence according to aesthetic considerations such as texture, colour, and mood.

I have worked as a photographer around the world, but this project has special significance for me, not simply because St Andrews is now where I live, but because my father came here on a bursary from a mining town in Fife and it changed his life; and by extension my own. Being at St Andrews University opened his eyes to a world of possibilities, and that sense of worldliness was the greatest gift he could pass on to his offspring. After gaining a PhD from Imperial College, my father returned to the town to receive his DSc and brought his family here on holiday when we were children. While I was not born in St Andrews, the connection I feel to the place is deep and enduring.

Fergus Wilkie

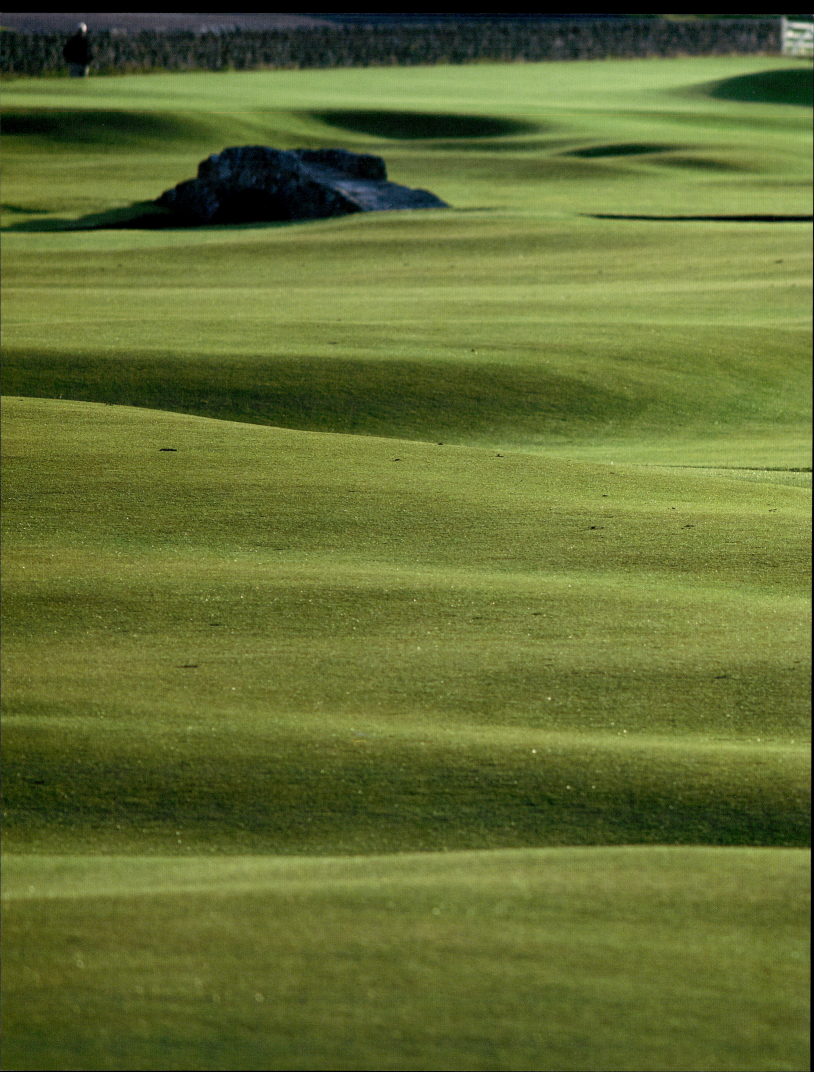

HENRY WARDLAW

Bishop of St Andrews
1403 – 1440

Fundator Loci

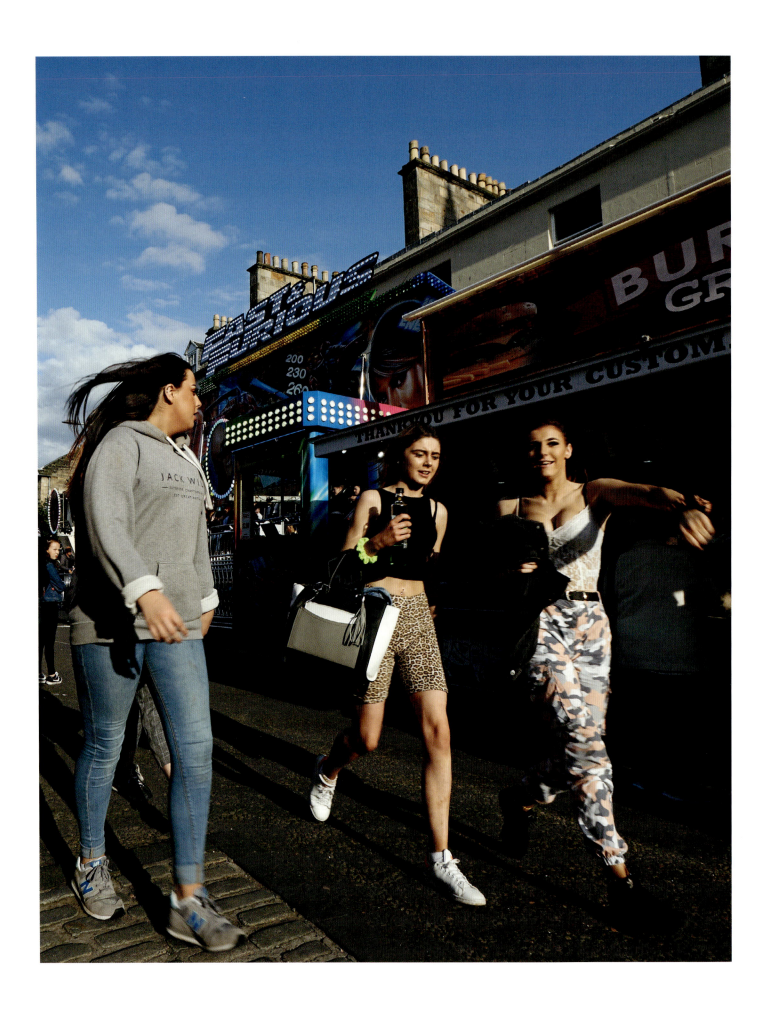

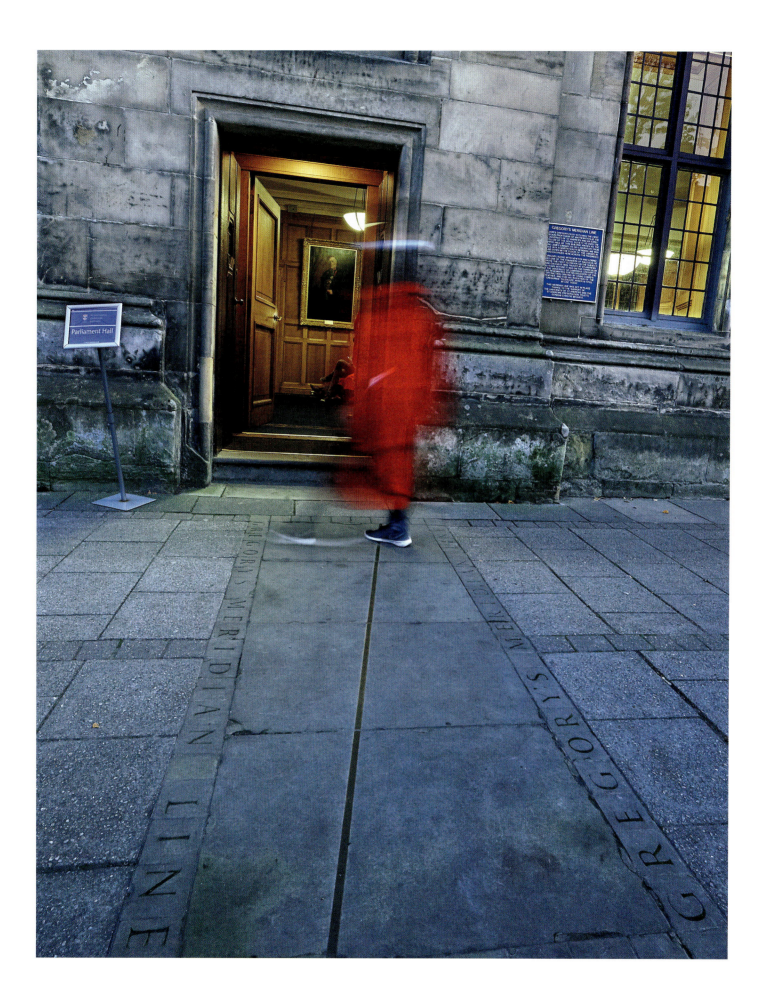

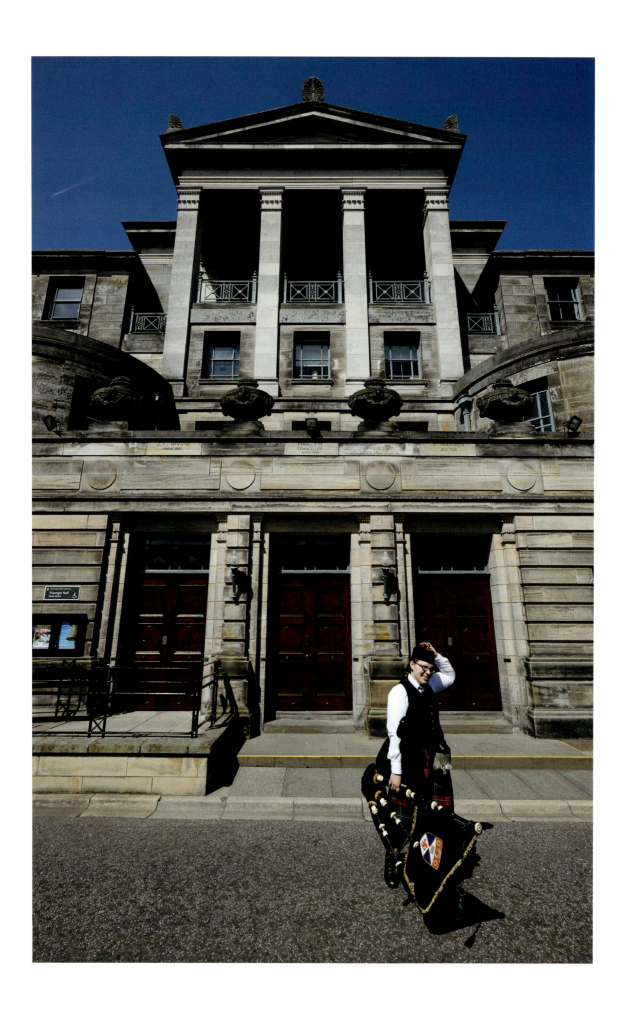

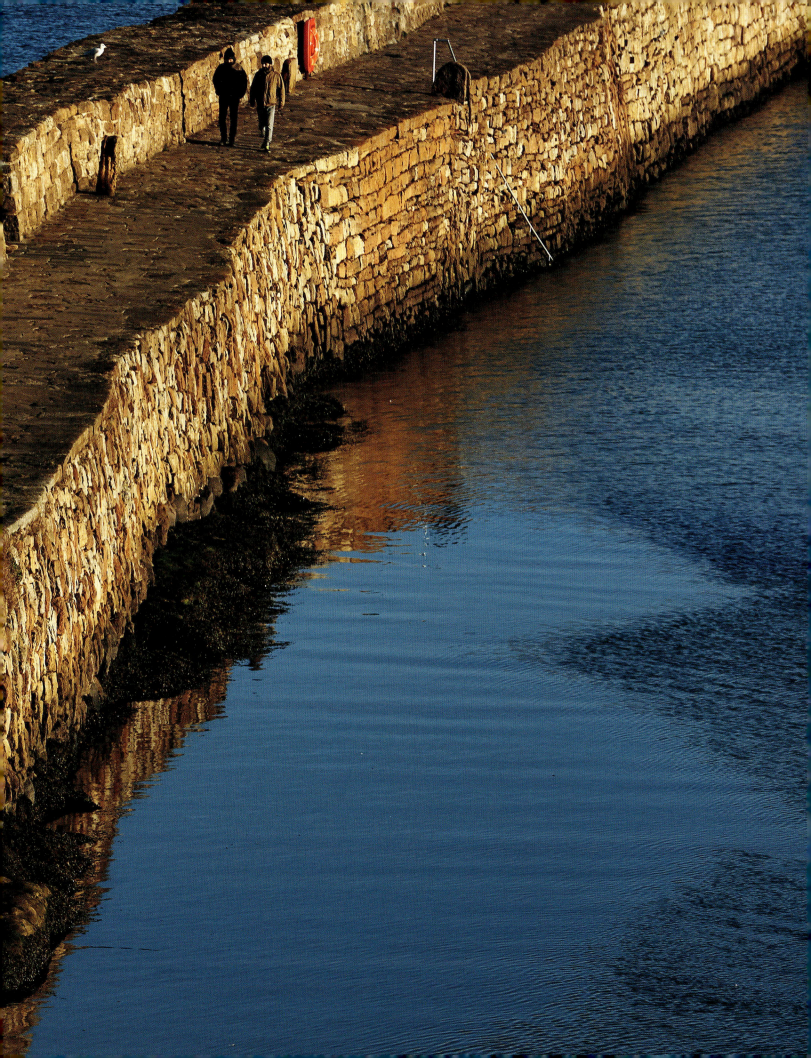

2-3 The wide fairways of the first and last holes of the Old Course are adjacent to the town, seen from the west. A small crowd gathers at the 18th green to watch the final strokes of a play-off for the St Andrews Links Trophy, an annual competition for amateurs.

6-7 View of Out Head and St Andrews Links from the Eden Estuary. This grass-covered sandy headland to the north-west of the town is home to five 18-hole golf courses and a nine-hole course. In the foreground is the Jubilee Course, opened in 1897.

8-9 A moment for reflection standing on Elephant Rock, which offers a good vantage point across the expanse of the West Sands at low tide.

16-17 A group of young people enjoys a summer evening stroll on the West Sands as a flock of seagulls takes to the air. Offshore, a sailing ship makes a rare appearance in St Andrews Bay, dropping anchor for one night.

18-19 Strong offshore winds, a dry beach and low tide combine to create the rare visual phenomenon of loose sand blowing in streaks from the dunes across the West Sands. A woman takes the opportunity to photograph her dog in strange surroundings.

20-21 Looking vertically down on the West Sands where the Swilken Burn meanders towards the North Sea.

28-29 Dogs and their walkers appear insignificant amid the vast expanse and shimmering ripples of the West Sands.

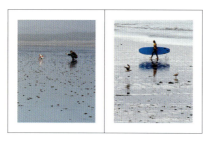

30 A toddler is curious about lugworm castings and burrows, as Dad looks on.

31 End of a surfing session on the glistening West Sands with only gulls for company.

32 Eye to eye across the Step Rock Tidal Pool, one of many public open air pools across Scotland that have fallen into disuse.
33 Time to chill atop Elephant Rock on a late summer's evening, overlooking West Sands.

40-41 St Andrews in profile glows in the warm evening light, adorned by a dramatic sky and its reflection on the West Sands.

42-43 Summer sunset, West Sands.

44-45 Mysterious semblance at the strand, as the blue hour gets under way.

10-11 Surfing beginners head out to the waves under the supervision of the Blown Away Surf School based at the West Sands.

12-13 A young boy watches his toy truck float along the Swilken Burn as it flows across the West Sands into the North Sea.

14-15 Sunset on the deserted West Sands seems to be the perfect time for a mother to run along leading her daughter on a pony.

22-23 Young people find a meeting point with a view on Elephant Rock as waves roll in off the North Sea onto the West Sands.

24-25 A woman evinces a sense of being carefree while two other women take a selfie a little further out into the water.

26-27 In a spray-filled seascape, a man seems to be suspended in mid-air as he runs across the water into the surf.

34-35 Two undergraduates in traditional red gowns converse with a photographer as small waves ripple onto the West Sands.

36-37 Separate stories play out on the wet sands of a receding tide, in what seem like four quarters of a blank canvas.

38-39 Early morning autumn swimmers race across the low-tide expanse of the West Sands, as a small haar sits just offshore.

46-47 Partial eclipse of a full moon rising over the castle and cathedral during the blue hour. Ladies Lake, the modern home on the clifftop, replaced a 1960s dwelling and has won several architectural and technology awards since completion in 2016.

48-49 The Old Course winds its distinctive hook-shaped path from the town to the Eden Estuary, wrapping around a nub of the New Course (1895), mostly on the left. The Jubilee Course (1897) is beyond on the far side. The Eden Course (1914) is on the right.

50-51 The final putt of the professional part of the Alfred Dunhill Links Championship, a pro-am tournament that has a pro winner and a pro-am team winner. The final round is played on the Old Course, after three rounds at Carnoustie, Kingsbarns and St Andrews.

52 Pipe smokers take in the view over the 18th green in front of The Royal & Ancient Golf Club of St Andrews clubhouse.
53 Former England cricketer Kevin Pietersen signs autographs after his pro-am round in the Alfred Dunhill Links Championship.

54 Iconic view of the Swilken Bridge and The Royal & Ancient Golf Club clubhouse on the 18th hole of the Old Course.
55 The Swilken Bridge provides plenty of photo opportunities, not only for golfers but non-golfers too, especially on Sundays.

56-57 Two local players observe social distancing while waiting for their tee time at the entrance to the first hole of the Old Course. Restricted play started after three months of closure at the outbreak of the Covid-19 coronavirus pandemic in Spring 2020.

64-65 Dunes and gorse bushes common to links golf courses loom behind a player on the 11th hole of the New Course.

66-67 Player and caddy search for a lost ball in the rough of the 17th fairway of the Old Course. Hamilton Grand, a block of luxury apartments, dominates the view. It opened as the Grand Hotel in 1895 and was a hall of residence, Hamilton Hall, from 1949 to 2006.

68 People walk the Old Course on a Sunday, when golf is not played due to a 16th century edict still observed today to rest the grass.
69 Players on the 17th green and 18th tee can almost feel the breath of passers-by on Old Station Road, running right alongside.

76-77 Golfers make use of a ramp with steps down the middle to get their golf trolleys off the Old Course at the end of a round and onto the path in front of The Royal & Ancient Golf Club clubhouse.

78-79 Playing partners react to a putt that sits on the lip of the 18th hole of the Old Course, while a couple strolls on the fairway seemingly oblivious to the fact that play is in progress. The Old Course Hotel and the Jigger Inn can be seen in the background.

80-81 The last four-ball of the day is a riot of colour and traditional garb, the clubhouse clock timing the last putts at 10.43pm.

88-89 Kingdom Brass from Kelty, Fife, are one of the brass bands that travel to play at St Andrews bandstand during the summer. The band was First Section National Champion at the National Championship of Great Britain in Cheltenham in 2021.

90-91 Flowers beds at The Scores near the Martyrs' Monument, overlooking the North Sea. The town has been named best coastal town in Britain at the Royal Horticultural Society's Britain in Bloom Awards.

92 A volunteer for St Andrews in Bloom tends to tulips in Market Street. Volunteers place planters and baskets all around town.
93 A judge for the caber toss, the Scottish hammer throw and other heavy weight events at St Andrews Highland Games.

58-59 A two-ball game gets under way as the players walk down the first fairway in front of the clubhouse of Royal & Ancient Golf Club. The club's role as one of golf's governing bodies was spun off in 2004 into a new organisation called The R&A.

60-61 St Andrews Links clubhouse sits at the foot of the New and Jubilee courses. In the foreground are the early and late parts of the Old Course, including the famous 17th "road" hole, whose green lies alongside the road leading to the old Links railway station.

62-63 Young golfers on the elevated tee of the 11th "high (in)" hole on the Old Course, a par 3 often described as the shortest par 5 in Scotland, due to the brutality of its bunkers and sloping green.

70-71 A typical Sunday scene on the Old Course when there is no golf and the public takes full advantage to stroll or walk the dog.

72-73 A golf balls whizzes past the nose of a dog being led across Grannie Clark's Wynd, a public footpath traversing the 1st and 18th fairways of the Old Course. Walkers are advised to wait for a break in play but sometimes get their timing wrong.

74-75 A spring tide at high tide shows how close the Old Course is to the West Sands. Golfers size up their putts on the 18th green.

82-83 Golf Place is home to two of the town's famous names in golfing equipment. St Andrews Golf Co claims to be the last club maker in the world retaining traditional skills, while 125-year-old Auchterlonies is one of the most iconic names in the game.

84-85 The Martyrs' Monument dates from 1843 and is an important landmark as it commemorates four Protestants, including Patrick Hamilton, executed for their beliefs in the run-up to the Scottish Reformation, a shift from the papacy to Presbyterianism.

86-87 A newly married couple having their wedding photographs done at sunset in the shadow of the Martyrs' Monument, a famous landmark in a prominent location on The Scores near The Royal & Ancient clubhouse.

94-95 At the St Andrews Highland Games, the winner of one of the Highland Dancing categories is interviewed by a French television documentary crew, while family members and other contestants look on.

96-97 Contestants in one of the Highland Dancing categories line up before going onto the stage at St Andrews Highland Games.

98-99 Solo Piping, as distinct from band piping, is an important part of any highland games, and this contestant does his best to impress the judge with his bagpipe playing.

100-101 The sign at St Andrews bus station is a familiar sight to regular travellers.

102-103 The best preserved city gate in Scotland, according to the body responsible for its upkeep, Historic Environment Scotland, the West Port was constructed in 1587 as a monumental entrance to South Street. It was extensively refurbished in 1843.

104-105 The ruins of Blackfriars Chapel sit in front of the original Madras College on busy South Street. The chapel was built in the 1520s as an addition to the church of the Dominican Friars, built 10 years earlier, and destroyed by Protestant reformers in 1559.

112-113 South Street boasts some of the oldest buildings, grandest properties, and interesting architecture in St Andrews.

114-115 Janettas Gelateria is a St Andrews institution and an obligatory stop on the visitor itinerary. Founded in 1908 by Italian Bennett Janetta, who had arrived in Fife from a village in Lazio, the business is now run by his great-granddaughter and her husband.

116-117 The biggest, boldest cone with everything on it! The parents of the current Jannettas owner grew the business in the 1970s into the modern operation, expanding the range of flavours to 52, probably the most in Scotland at the time.

124-125 The Lammas Fair or Lammas Market is an annual street market and fair that dates to medieval times, taking place in the five days up to the second Tuesday in August, initially only in Market Street before expanding for the last two days.

126 The streets of St Andrews are taken over for a few days during the Lammas Fair.

127 You are never too young for the Lammas Fair at the end of the summer holidays.

128 Iain R Spink sells his Arbroath smokies at St Andrews farmers' market. The haddock must be prepared using traditional methods close to Arbroath to claim protected status.

129 The Lammas Fair is a time to stroll along the streets to take in the atmosphere.

136-137 An undergraduate student wearing a traditional red gown walks along Butts Wynd, next to St Salvator's Quad. Red gowns can be worn by students of all schools, without any obligation, except St Mary's College, which has its own variation.

138-139 The University Chaplain and the Principal & Vice-Chancellor come in from the rain at the end of Sunday service at St Salvator's Chapel. The church lies at the historic heart of the town and dates from 1450, a rare example of Late Medieval architecture.

140-141 Winter sunlight shines across the cobbles of College Street, a busy conduit.

106-107 Cherry blossom on one of 1,000 trees donated in 1973 by Zenya Hamada as thanks for consenting to his New St Andrews Golf Club in Japan. First a Nicklaus-designed course, a member buy-out later added an Old Course-inspired short course.

108-109 A bronze statue of Henry Wardlaw, Bishop of St Andrews (1403-1440) and founder and first chancellor of the university, dominates the quad of St Mary's College. The statue was unveiled in 2013.

110-111 Lower Parliament Hall, or simply Parliament Hall, rarely seen with an unobstructed view, is part of St Mary's College and one of the university's historic buildings. It is so named because the Scots Parliament convened here from 1645 to 1646.

118-119 Young participants in St Andrews' Line in the Sand protest join adults to form a huge line of people on the West Sands, part of the worldwide Climate Change Strike organised by Extinction Rebellion.

120-121 The Lammas Fair or Lammas Market is an annual street market and fair that dates to medieval times, taking place over five days up to the second Tuesday in August, reaching South Street for the last two days. Today it is primarily a fun fair.

122-123 The Lammas Fair or Lammas Market is an annual street market and fair that dates to medieval times. There is a fun fair, continental market, food and drink, and other stalls. The Lammas Fair portends the last embers of the school summer holidays.

130-131 The Lammas Fair or Lammas Market, dating to medieval times, is thought to be the oldest street fair in Scotland. At the fun fair, assembled in a tight space, modern rides like this one in South Street are juxtaposed with ancient buildings.

132-133 The Lammas Fair or Lammas Market is an annual jamboree that takes over Market Street and South Street with noisy fun and thrills. At nighttime the fun fair comes alive for older participants. For many, it marks the last hurrah of the summer.

134 Waiting on the corner of Butts Wynd.

135 St Salvator's Tower on North Street.

142-143 Many of the old buildings in the centre of St Andrews were built with stones plundered from the cathedral after it had been ransacked by a Protestant mob in 1559, abandoned and fallen into ruin. This stonework is now tended by specialists.

144-145 Silhouettes against the backdrop of ancient stonework in South Castle Street, with a view along to the castle ruins.

146-147 Four children are taken to school in a cargo bike along Market Street, passing by the Whyte-Melville Memorial Fountain, built in 1881 in memory of Major George Whyte-Melville, a locally born novelist, by public subscription at the instigation of his mother.

148-149 The Kate Kennedy Procession is an annual university tradition originating in the adoration by students of the niece of Bishop Kennedy, founder of St Salvator's College. Kate, the most beautiful woman of her day, is played by a first-year male student.

150 An undergraduate adjusts her gown in blustery conditions at the pier.
151 An gowned undergraduate steps over Gregory's Meridian at Parliament Hall, where the union debating society meets. Gregory's Meridian pre-dates the Greenwich Meridian.

152-153 The pier walk is a Sunday tradition. After the service at St Salvator's Chapel, and at other times, students proceed to the end of the pier and back. It is not obligatory to own a gown but it offers the opportunity to get immersed in the culture of the university.

160-161 Medical graduates celebrate with friends and families in St Salvator's Quad after the summer graduation ceremony.

162-163 Newly conferred postgraduates in St Salvator's Quad after the summer graduation awards ceremony and parade.

164-165 A proud parent and his graduate son linger in St Salvator's Quad after the summer graduation ceremony and parade on their way to the graduation garden party.

172-173 The Purple Man of St Andrews is a local character who is often seen around town wearing only purple – from his shoes to his beard! Here he passes by the Roundel and The Pends Gate, the 14th-century main entrance into the cathedral precinct.

174 The view along South College Street towards the castle ruins.

175 A girl leads her dog through The Eye of the Needle, a side entrance to The Pends Gate leading onto The Pends (street) itself.

176-177 St Andrews Castle has played an important role in the religious and political history of Scotland. It has been home to kings and has served as a bishop's palace, fortress and state prison. What we see today are the ruins of a castle rebuilt circa 1400.

184-185 Pigeons take flight from the façade of the castle ruins at sunrise.

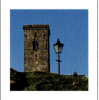

186 An aerial view of the castle ruins from St Andrews Bay.
187 St Rule's Tower was built circa 1123 by Celtic monks, the Culdees, about 40 years before the cathedral. They were soon ousted as Scotland shifted to the Roman church.

188-189 Sunrise over the cathedral. Pilgrims came from around Europe to see the relics that give the town its name, the bones of St Andrew. Its demise came with the Scottish Reformation, when Scotland broke with Rome and formed the Calvinist Kirk.

154-155 After the pier walk at the start of the Martinmas semester, the biggest walk of the year, undergraduates in traditional red gowns make their way back to town past the cathedral ruins. Gowns are knee-length, made from pure wool with a velvetine collar.

156 A piper awaits the end of a graduation awards ceremony at Younger Hall to lead the graduation parade to St Salvator's Quad.
157 The Chancellor and Vice-Chancellor of the university enter St Salvator's Quad at the head of a summer graduation parade.

158-159 The University Chaplain enters St Salvator's Quad as part of the graduation parade that leads from Younger Hall, after a summer graduation awards ceremony.

166-167 Doctorate and Masters graduates parade around St Salvator's Quad in the spiralling pattern of the traditional graduation procession after receiving their degrees at one of the winter graduation ceremonies.

168-169 A PhD graduate from the School of Medicine celebrates with his family from Malawi in St Salvator's Quad after the winter graduation procession. The red gown is not a St Andrews one, but a graduation gown from the University of KwaZulu-Natal.

170-171 Remembrance Day in St Andrews is observed each year with a military pipe band marching through the streets before and after a ceremony at the War Memorial, which is located at the end of North Street next to the walls of the cathedral.

178-179 Many Protestants were imprisoned and persecuted here during the Scottish Reformation, but it later became their refuge until defeat at the hands of a French fleet. The top of the notorious bottle dungeon can be seen in the lawn of the castle.

180-181 The sun goes down over the castle ruins. Deprived of any function following the success of the Scottish Reformation, the castle had fallen into such disrepair by 1656 that the burgh council ordered the use of its materials to repair the pier.

182-183 The blue hour adds a sense of calm to the view from the pier to the castle and out into St Andrews Bay.

190-191 Early morning view of St Andrews Cathedral. Built between 1168 and 1318, its consecration was attended by the king, Robert the Bruce. It was the centre of the medieval Roman Catholic church and one of the most celebrated cathedrals in Europe.

192-193 In a seaside town, gulls can be a nuisance, but sometimes they form an impressive flock.

194-195 The largest building in Scotland, the cathedral was ransacked by a Protestant mob in 1559 in the Scottish Reformation. The interior was destroyed and the cathedral declined, falling into ruin as it became a source of building material for the town.

196-197 St Andrews Cathedral must have been a spectacular sight for anyone arriving by sea, and it remains a prominent landmark even in its ruined state. Only in 1826, after years of being plundered for stones, did preservation of the stonework begin.

198-199 Aerial view of St Andrews from the east on a calm, clear morning, sweeping from the harbour in the foreground, past the cathedral, castle and historic centre, to the links in the distance. The tiny figure of a paddle boarder is seen in St Andrews Bay.

200-201 The main section of the pier (properly long or north pier) was built in 1656 using stones from the ruins of the cathedral and castle, replacing the original pier that was damaged in a storm the previous year. It affords a popular walk to the end and back.

208-209 The pastel coloured buildings on the tidal harbour belie its history as a busy port trading mainly with the low countries. It thrived on fishing, handling farm produce and coal and, later, leisure trips. Passenger services operated to Dundee and Leith.

210-211 A dense haar, or cold sea fog, is captured on camera as it retreats rapidly from the harbour at high tide. Haars occur most frequently on the north-east coast of Britain between April and September when warm air passes over the cold North Sea.

212-213 A lobster fisherman wheels his creels (traps) along the quayside. The harbour is integral to the history of the town, having been established in the 12th century. Piers were added in the 16th century and by the 19th century it was at its peak.

220 Fourth-year students (magistrands), who wear the gown off both shoulders, over the elbows, take an evening walk on the pier.
221 First year students (bejants) wear the gown fully up on the shoulders. Footwear is is not always such a conventional choice.

222-223 A low neap tide exposes a bank of soft sand at the extreme end of the East Sands, providing fun for dogs that want an easy dig. The Kinness Burn flows out to sea through the tidal harbour and past the pier.

224-225 A woman strikes the "one-legged wheel" yoga pose at sunrise on a calm May morning at St Andrews pier.

232-233 In a world of colour, nature can sometimes throw up a monochrome scene.

234-235 Shapes, textures and red wellies on the East Sands.

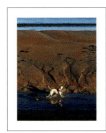 

236 Patterns and textures on the beach at the East Sands vary from day to day.

237 Ripples on the East Sands looking towards the harbour and cathedral.

202-203 The inner harbour forms a basin at the mouth of the Kinness Burn at high tide or when the sluice gates between the outer and inner harbours are closed. This creates better conditions in heavy weather for the growing number of pleasure craft.

204-205 Houses are reflected in the calm water of a high spring tide, as a heron takes flight over the harbour. St Andrews is still a working port with a small but thriving lobster industry supplying St Andrews Bay lobster to the top restaurants in town and beyond.

206-207 The long pier and cross pier form the sheltered haven of the outer harbour. A low neap tide exposes the depth of the stonework and reveals the Kinness Burn where it discharges into the North Sea at the northern end of the East Sands.

214-215 Lobsters can be bought on the quayside directly from boats such as Excel KY79. Once booming on the likes of herring, the fishing industry declined at the outbreak of World War II. Now it is limited to exploiting the lobster catch in St Andrews Bay.

216 Occasionally high winds will play havoc with long hair.
217 Jumping from the end of pier on a Sunday afternoon is a favourite activity of the adventurous.

218-219 The pier walk is a university tradition that persists on all but the coldest Sundays of the year. After the service at St Salvator's Chapel, students proceed to the end of the pier and back, often clad in undergraduate red gowns.

226-227 Alpacas from Bowbridge Farm at Peat Inn near St Andrews engage the crowds at the summer Harbour Gala adjacent to the East Sands.

228 A brave and energetic dog fetches any stick from any wave in any temperature.

229 Laughing at Grannie's misfortune, a boy escapes a breaking wave on the East Sands.

230-231 Glistening water left by a receding tide creates an impressionistic scene.

238-239 The sweeping view across the East Sands towards the harbour and cathedral.

240-241 Early morning view towards St Andrews from Maiden Rock (aka Maiden's Rock), a sandstone sea stack at Kinkell Braes, created by wave erosion about 6,500 years ago when its base lay at sea level.

242-243 A member of St Andrews University Mountaineering Club get to grips with Buddo Rock, a sandstone sea stack on a raised beach. This stunning rock formation is on the Fife Coastal Path near Boarhills.

Acknowledgements

Many thanks to the following people and organisations, whose contributions have made this book possible or have enriched the experience of producing it.

Soulla Petrou; Neil Shaw; Karla Smith; Vadim Wilkie; my siblings Deborah, Nigel and Edwin; Suzanne Deas; Pamela Dove; Zahid Siddique; Sue Azam-Ali; Peter Adamson; Desiree Finlayson; Ella Yip; Jasmine Laws; Sami Azam-Ali; Neil Macpherson Shaw; Hamish King; Sharyn Emslie; Clare Krabbe; Ken Dalton; Marjorie Dalton; Colin MacDonald; Margaret MacDonald; Rev Dr Donald MacEwan; Neil Winter; Hannah Weir; Beth McConnochie; Kate Gilbertson; Hilary Scott; Iain Spink; Jenni Alexander; St Andrews Links; the University of St Andrews; Jannettas; Historic Environment Scotland; Leuchars Air Traffic Control.

The Photographer

Fergus Wilkie was born in a village in Cumbria, north-west England, in 1962, to a father from Buckhaven, Fife, and a mother from Perthshire. He spent his childhood holidays in Scotland connecting with his relatives and Scottish culture, a connection so strong that at 18 he chose between two Scottish universities, St Andrews and Edinburgh. The draw of the big city was the greater, but St Andrews bided its time and in 2015 Fergus became a resident of the town.

With a career that could be characterised as unusually diverse, Fergus began adult life as the best French speaker his school had known, but he eschewed languages in higher education to complete an honours degree in mechanical engineering. Technical journalism beckoned, but within a few years Fergus found his way to the Financial Times as a sub-editor at the age of 26. It was an exciting time to be working in the newsroom of a daily newspaper, feeling the pulse of tumultuous world events such as the fall of the Berlin Wall and the end of Apartheid.

It was while at the FT that Fergus made the transition to photography. He had always been keen on the craft, borrowing his father's cameras at a young age and even asking, somewhat cheekily, at the age of 9 or 10, if he might inherit all the equipment when his father died!

The FT was experiencing a golden era of picture usage under its then news editor. Fergus worked as a picture editor and photographer, but it was not long before sweeping changes blew through the FT news team, especially the picture desk, which was disbanded in favour of a new structure.

Thrown into the deep end as a freelance photographer, Fergus continued to work for the FT but also took commissions from newspapers such as the Financial Mail, The Scotsman and Sunday Times; and for the big City of London financial PR firms, with work published widely in the nationals, including The Guardian, The Times, Daily Telegraph and Independent. He also turned his hand to colour magazines, as well as shooting stills for film productions.

Fergus moved on to high-end commissions in the Caribbean for a British publisher, shooting portraits and scenery, and this became a significant part of his career. When not hanging out of helicopters over the Blue Mountains of Jamaica or the turquoise waters of Exuma in The Bahamas, he was photographing politicians, business people and celebrities, such as Sean Connery, Sydney Poitier, Usain Bolt, Rita Marley and Bunny Wailer.

The route to St Andrews has not been merely a physical one. With echoes of the pilgrimages of old, this project has brought a sense of homecoming to the Kingdom of Fife.

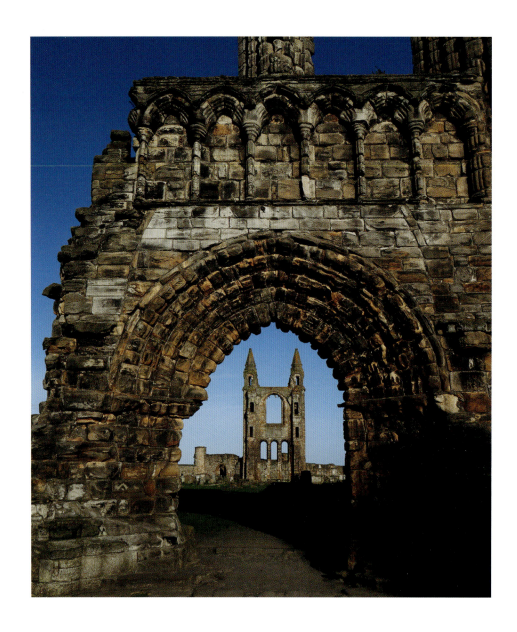

Published in Scotland by Fototank
54 South Street, St Andrews, Fife KY16 9JT
www.fototank.com   standrews@fototank.com

Printed and bound in Italy by Printer Trento
ISBN 978-1-7398106-0-3